Omelettes Pancakes &Fritters

KÖNEMANN

Waffles

Waffles are a simple way to end a meal or a delicious treat on their own. Choose different shapes and sizes from the variety available in supermarkets, delicatessens and department stores. Or make your own to serve with our indulgent sauces.

Waffle Batter

Into a medium bowl, sift ¼ cup self-raising flour, 1½ cups plain flour and 2 tablespoons sugar. Make a well in the centre. In a jug, combine 1 teaspoon vanilla, 50 g melted butter, 1¼ cups milk and 2 egg yolks, reserving whites. Add to flour and whisk until batter is smooth and free of any lumps. Beat 2 egg whites until soft peaks form. Using a metal spoon, fold egg whites into the batter until smooth. Spoon the mixture, 2–3 tablespoons at a time, onto lightly greased preheated waffle iron or maker. Close lid and cook 2–3 minutes or until waffles are golden and cooked through. Serve immediately with your favourite sauce and ice-cream or cream.

Sauces, clockwise from left: Rich Chocolate, Walnut & Maple Syrup, Ginger Lime Syrup, Sweet Custard, Berry, Caramel Butterscotch.

Sweet Custard Sauce

In a small pan, combine 2 tablespoons golden syrup, 2 tablespoons caster sugar, 1 tablespoon custard powder, ½ cup milk and 1 cup cream. Stir over medium heat until mixture boils and thickens. Allow mixture to cool slightly before serving over waffles with fresh strawberries and ice-cream.

Rich Chocolate Sauce

Combine 100 g chopped dark chocolate, ½ cup cream, 40 g butter and 1 tablespoon golden syrup in a small pan. Stir over medium heat until chocolate and butter are melted and mixture is smooth. If desired, add 1–2 tablespoons chocolate or coffee liqueur to mixture. Sauce may be served warm or cold over waffles and ice-cream.

Caramel Butterscotch Sauce

Combine 80 g butter, 1/4 cup soft brown sugar, 1 cup cream and 2 tablespoons golden syrup in a small pan. Stir over medium heat without boiling, until butter is melted and sugar has dissolved. Stir for another 2 minutes or until sauce darkens slightly. Add 2 tablespoons condensed milk for a richer sauce. Serve hot over waffles and ice-cream or mascarpone cheese.

Berry Sauce

Combine 2/3 cup water, 2/3 cup caster sugar, 2 tablespoons lemon juice and 2 cinnamon sticks in a medium pan. Stir over medium heat, without boiling, until sugar has dissolved. Add 250 g punnet of raspberries and one of blueberries. Bring to boil, reduce heat and simmer 2–3 minutes. Add 125 g raspberries and stir gently until just heated through. Add 1 tablespoon Cointreau or kirsch if desired. Serve warm or cold.

Walnut & Maple Syrup Sauce

Combine 60 g butter, 2 tablespoons soft brown sugar, 1/4 cup maple syrup and 1/4 cup sour cream in a small pan. Stir over medium heat until sugar has dissolved and mixture is smooth. Stir in 1/4 cup toasted walnut halves and stir until heated through. Sauce may be served over waffles and ice-cream.

Ginger Lime Syrup

In a small pan, combine 2 tablespoons ginger and lime marmalade, 1/4 cup finely sliced ginger in syrup (including the syrup), 1 tablespoon each of soft brown sugar and caster sugar, 1 cup water and the shredded rind of 1 lime. Stir over medium heat until sugar dissolves. Reduce heat and simmer, uncovered, 5–10 minutes or until mixture has reduced and thickened slightly.

Omelettes

To make a good omelette, it is best to work quickly so, before you begin, have your ingredients prepared and utensils ready. The savoury recipes make a tasty, nutritious light meal on their own or may be combined with salads or vegetables. The sweet omelettes are suitable for dessert or a snack.

Omelette with Pizza Topping

Preparation time:
  20 minutes
Total cooking time:
  15 minutes
Serves 4

2 tablespoons olive oil
1 onion, thinly sliced
1/2 red capsicum, cut
  into thin strips
5 eggs
1/4 cup milk
salt and pepper
1/2 cup grated
  mozzarella or cheddar
  cheese
1 stick cabanossi,
  sliced
6 black olives, pitted,
  sliced
1/4 teaspoon dried
  oregano or
  1 tablespoon chopped
  fresh oregano

1. Heat 1 tablespoon oil in non-stick pan. Add onion and capsicum. Stir over medium heat 5 minutes or until soft. Remove from pan; drain on paper towels.
2. Combine eggs, milk, salt and pepper in medium mixing bowl. Beat with a wire whisk for 2 minutes. Heat remaining oil in same non-stick pan. Pour egg mixture into pan and shake pan to spread mixture evenly over base; cook for 1 minute over medium-high heat without stirring.
3. Remove pan from heat. Preheat grill to high. Sprinkle partly cooked omelette with onion and capsicum mixture, cheese, cabanossi and olives. Sprinkle with oregano.

Omelette with Pizza Topping.

4. Cook pizza-topped omelette under preheated grill for 3 minutes or until eggs are just firm and cheese is bubbling.

Note: Be careful that you do not place the handle of the pan directly beneath heat source.

Noodle Omelette

Preparation time:
  10 minutes
Total cooking time:
  13 minutes
Serves 6

85 g packet chicken
  flavoured instant
  noodles
3/4 cup water
4 eggs, lightly beaten
1 tablespoon oil
1/3 cup grated cheddar
  cheese
100 g stick peperoni
  sausage, thinly sliced

1. Place instant noodles, contents of flavouring sachet and water in a small pan. Bring to the boil, reduce heat, simmer, covered, for 5 minutes. Remove from heat, remove lid and allow noodles to absorb any remaining liquid.
2. Combine noodles and beaten eggs in a large mixing bowl; mix

well. Heat oil in a large non-stick frying pan over medium heat. Preheat grill to high.
3. Add noodle mixture to pan, shake pan to spread mixture evenly over base. Cook for 5 minutes without stirring; remove pan from heat.
4. Sprinkle omelette with grated cheese and sliced sausage; place under grill. Cook for 3 minutes or until sausage is crisp and cheese has melted. Serve with lettuce and sliced tomato, if desired.

Plain French Omelette

Preparation time:
  5 minutes
Total cooking time:
  2 minutes
Serves 1–2

3 eggs
2 tablespoons water
salt and pepper
30 g butter

1. Place eggs, water, salt and pepper in medium

mixing bowl. Using a fork, beat mixture for 2 minutes.
2. Place butter in small non-stick pan and heat over high heat. When butter is foaming, add egg mixture all at once.
3. Swirl mixture with back of a fork several times. Cook over high heat until eggs are almost set, tilting pan and lifting egg edges occasionally to allow uncooked egg to flow underneath.
4. Fold omelette in half, tilt pan and slide omelette onto a warm plate for serving. Serve with salad greens and sliced onion, if desired.

Hint
To make an easy variation, sprinkle omelette with shredded ham and freshly grated gruyère cheese before folding OR serve omelette with the traditional French vegetable casserole known as ratatouille. Plain French Omelette is delicious served with fresh crusty French bread and tossed green salad or steamed vegetables.

---

*French Omelette with Ham and Cheese variation
(top) and Noodle Omelette.*

Savoury Omelette Rolls

Preparation time:
  15 minutes
Total cooking time:
  10 minutes
Makes 5

4 eggs
2 tablespoons water
2 teaspoons soy sauce
2 teaspoons peanut oil

1. Place eggs, water and sauce in medium mixing bowl. Beat with a wire whisk for 2 minutes.
2. Brush base of a small non-stick pan with oil. Heat pan on high. Pour one-fifth of egg mixture into base of pan. Shake pan to spread mixture evenly over base. Heat for 20 seconds or until egg has almost set. Remove pan from heat. Using an egg slice, or large flat-bladed knife, roll omelette from one end forming a roll. Transfer to warm plate; cover with a tea-towel.
3. Repeat process with remaining egg mixture, using one-fifth of the mixture each time.

Note: For extra flavour, before rolling, spread omelettes with a pesto or olive paste or other filling of your choice. Roll up tightly and cut into rounds for serving.

Prawn Omelettes

Preparation time:
  10 minutes
Total cooking time:
  12 minutes
Serves 4–5 (Makes 20)

Sauce
2/3 cup bottled plum
  sauce
2 spring onions, finely
  chopped
1 teaspoon brown
  vinegar

6 eggs, lightly beaten
200 g can peeled
  prawns, drained
1/2 cup fresh bean
  sprouts, chopped
1 teaspoon soy sauce
1 teaspoon hoi sin sauce
1 teaspoon sesame oil
pinch five spice powder
1/4 cup oil

1. **To make sauce:** Beat plum sauce, chopped spring onion and vinegar in small bowl for 1 minute.
2. Place eggs, prawns, sprouts, sauces, sesame oil and spice into medium mixing bowl. Beat with a fork until all ingredients are combined.
3. Brush base of large non-stick or heavy-based pan with oil. Heat pan over low heat 2 minutes. Place 4 oiled egg rings on base of pan about 3–4 cm apart.

Spoon some mixture into each ring. Cover pan with a lid, cook omelettes over low heat for 2 minutes or until just set. Lift onto warm plate; remove rings. Cover omelettes with tea-towel, keep warm. Repeat process with remaining mixture, greasing pan and rings when necessary.
4. To serve omelettes, overlap 3–4 on serving plates; drizzle with sauce. Serve with shredded lettuce if desired.

Creamy Omelette

Preparation time:
  4 minutes
Total cooking time:
  3 minutes
Serves 2

3 eggs
1/4 cup cream
salt and pepper
20 g butter

1. Place eggs, cream, salt and pepper in medium mixing bowl. Beat with a wire whisk for 2 minutes.
2. Heat butter in a small non-stick pan over medium heat. When butter is foaming, add mixture to pan all at once; stir with wooden spoon for 15 seconds.

Clockwise from top left: Creamy Omelette, Savoury Omelette Rolls (Pesto and Olive Paste variations) and Prawn Omelettes.

3. Cook until mixture is almost set, tilting pan and lifting egg edges occasionally to allow uncooked egg to flow underneath. When almost set, fold omelette in half using an egg slice or flat-bladed knife. Centre of omelette should be moist and creamy. Alternatively, instead of folding the omelette, cooking process can be completed by covering pan with a lid for about 2 minutes. Serve sprinkled with fresh herbs and accompanied by sliced avocado, if desired.

9

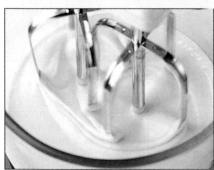

1. Beat egg mixture on high speed until it is creamy and a pale colour.

2. Add beaten egg whites to yolk mixture and fold in with a metal spoon.

Savoury Soufflé Omelette

Preparation time:
10 minutes
Total cooking time:
3 minutes
Serves 2–4

5 eggs, separated
2 teaspoons water
2 teaspoons lemon juice
salt and pepper
20 g butter
²/₃ cup coarsely grated
   cheddar cheese,
   optional

1. Place egg yolks, water, juice, salt and pepper in small mixing bowl. Using electric beaters, beat on high for 2 minutes or until mixture is pale and creamy.
2. Place egg whites in small, dry, mixing bowl. Using electric beaters or a wire whisk, beat egg whites until firm peaks form. Using a metal spoon, fold egg whites into yolk mixture. Preheat grill to high.
3. Place butter in deep non-stick pan and heat over high heat. When butter is foaming, add omelette mixture, swirl pan to spread evenly over base. Cook over high heat for 1 minute without stirring. Remove from heat; sprinkle with cheese.
4. Place under hot grill for 2–3 minutes or until omelette is puffed and golden. Sprinkle with chopped fresh herbs if desired.

Note: May be accompanied with grilled or sliced and pan-fried mushrooms or tomatoes which have been halved, sprinkled with cheese and grilled.

Savoury Soufflé Omelette.

3. Remove pan from heat and sprinkle grated cheese over top of omelette.

4. Soufflé omelette is cooked when it looks puffed and top is golden.

11

Herb Omelette

Preparation time:
  10 minutes
Total cooking time:
  5–6 minutes
Serves 2

4 eggs
1/4 cup milk
1 tablespoon sour
  cream
salt and pepper
1 tablespoon finely
  chopped fresh parsley
2 teaspoons chopped
  fresh chives
1 teaspoon shredded
  fresh mint
20 g butter
2 rashers bacon or
  4 slices of salami,
  chopped and fried,
  optional
tomato salsa, optional

1. Place eggs, milk, sour cream, salt, pepper, parsley, chives and mint in medium mixing bowl. Beat with a wire whisk 2 minutes or until well combined.
2. Place butter in large non-stick pan and heat over medium heat. When butter is foaming, pour egg mixture into pan, swirl mixture with the back of a fork several times.
3. Reduce heat to low, cook omelette for 5 minutes or until mixture begins to set, tilting pan and lifting egg edges occasionally to allow uncooked egg to flow underneath. Remove from heat. Tilt pan and slide omelette onto a warm plate, cut omelette into wedges.
4. Arrange pieces overlapping on serving plate. If desired, sprinkle omelette with crispy chopped, fried bacon or salami and a tomato salsa. Lettuce may be served with it.

Note: Alternatively, omelette may be served with natural yoghurt and sprinkled with fresh basil leaves.

Spanish Omelette

Preparation time:
  20 minutes
Total cooking time:
  40 minutes
Serves 4–6

1 kg potatoes, peeled
salt
2 large red onions
50 g butter
2 tablespoons olive oil
1 clove garlic, crushed
2 tablespoons finely
  chopped fresh parsley
4 eggs, lightly beaten

1. Cut peeled potatoes into 1.5 cm cubes. Place in large pan with salt; cover with water. Bring to boil, cook uncovered 3 minutes. Remove pan from heat, allow to stand, covered, for 8 minutes or until potato is just tender; drain well.
2. Chop onions coarsely. Heat butter and oil in deep non-stick frying pan over medium heat. Add onion and garlic, cook 8 minutes, stirring occasionally. Add potato and cook for another 5 minutes. Remove vegetables with a slotted spoon, transfer to a large mixing bowl.
3. Add chopped parsley and beaten eggs; mix well. Pour mixture into hot frying pan, reduce heat to low, cook, covered, 10 minutes or until underside is golden. Brown top of omelette under hot grill if desired.

Note: Omelette may be served with olives, lettuce and slices of red onion and garnished with sprigs of fresh herbs. Add 1 extra egg to mixture if desired.

Herb Omelette (top) and Spanish Omelette.

Bacon and Mushroom Omelette

Preparation time:
10 minutes
Total cooking time:
15 minutes
Serves 4–6

2 tablespoons olive oil
375 g small
  mushrooms, quartered
4 rashers bacon,
  chopped
6 eggs
1/3 cup thick cream
1 tablespoon tomato
  paste
salt and pepper
2 teaspoons chopped
  fresh basil leaves
1/2 cup coarsely grated
  cheddar cheese

1. Heat oil in large heavy-based frying pan. Add mushrooms and bacon. Stir over medium heat for 8 minutes or until golden and almost all liquid is absorbed. Remove pan from heat.
2. Place eggs, cream, paste, salt, pepper, basil and cheese in medium mixing bowl. Beat with a wire whisk until ingredients are combined.
3. Return pan with mushroom mixture to heat. Pour egg mixture into pan; stir with wooden spoon for 15 seconds. Shake pan to spread mixture evenly over base of pan. Cook over medium heat for 5 minutes or until omelette has almost set. Place pan under preheated grill and cook 2–3 more minutes or until top is set. Cut into wedges and serve immediately.

Omelette Shreds in Fresh Tomato Sauce

Preparation time:
 25 minutes
Total cooking time:
 12 minutes
Serves 2

Tomato Sauce
3 ripe tomatoes, peeled
  and roughly chopped
1/2 teaspoon salt
1/2 teaspoon pepper
1 teaspoon sugar
2 tablespoons shredded
  fresh basil

4 eggs
2 teaspoons soy sauce
1/4 teaspoon white
  pepper
1 tablespoon water
light olive oil

1. *To make tomato sauce:* Cook tomatoes in small pan with salt, pepper and sugar for 5 minutes or until liquid has reduced and thickened. Add basil.
2. Using a wire whisk, beat eggs in a medium mixing bowl with soy, pepper and water.
3. Heat a lightly oiled small frying pan. Pour in sufficient mixture to cover base. Cook for a few seconds, tip onto a plate. Brush pan with more oil and repeat process to make 3 thin omelettes.
4. Place omelettes on top of each other, roll into a cylinder shape. Using a sharp knife, cut into fine shreds.
5. Reheat sauce. Add egg shreds, warm gently, stirring until covered with tomato. If desired, serve with extra fresh shredded basil and cracked pepper.

HINT
Serve omelette shreds accompanied by a salad or as a side dish with roast chicken. Omelette shreds can also be used in soups, added to stir-fries or served over salads.

---

*Omelette Shreds in Fresh Tomato Sauce (top)
and Bacon and Mushroom Omelette.*

Mixed Grated Vegetable Frittata

Preparation time:
  25 minutes
Total cooking time:
  18 minutes
Serves 2–4

¼ *cup olive oil*
1 *onion, finely chopped*
1 *small carrot, grated*
1 *small zucchini, grated*
1 *cup grated pumpkin*
⅓ *cup finely diced*
  Jarlsburg or cheddar
  cheese
½ *teaspoon salt*
½ *teaspoon ground*
  black pepper
5 *eggs*

1. Heat 2 tablespoons oil in frying pan, add onion and cook gently for 5 minutes or until soft. Add carrot, zucchini and pumpkin, cover pan and cook over low heat for 3 minutes. Transfer to a mixing bowl, cool. Stir in cheese, salt and pepper.
2. Beat eggs and add to vegetables.
3. Heat remaining oil in small frying pan. When oil is hot, add egg mixture to pan and shake pan to spread mixture evenly over base. Reduce heat to low, cook 3 minutes or until set almost all the way through. Tilt pan and lift edges occasionally to allow uncooked egg to flow underneath. Cut into wedges and serve immediately.

Avocado and Cheese Omelette

Preparation time:
  12 minutes
Total cooking time:
  15 minutes
Serves 2

2 *tablespoons olive oil*
1 *medium onion, finely*
  chopped
1 *teaspoon curry*
  powder
1 *medium avocado,*
  peeled, seed removed
4 *eggs*
2 *tablespoons milk*
½ *teaspoon salt*
¼ *teaspoon white*
  pepper
30 g *butter*
½ *cup grated gruyère,*
  Jarlsburg or cheddar
  cheese
2 *rashers bacon,*
  chopped and stir-fried,
  optional
2 *teaspoons sweet Thai*
  chilli sauce
1 *tablespoon water*

1. Heat oil in a pan, add onion and cook over medium heat until soft. Add curry powder, stir 1–2 minutes. Transfer to a bowl; cool. Chop avocado in 1 cm pieces and combine with cooled onion mixture.
2. Beat eggs with milk, salt and pepper. Preheat grill.
3. Melt butter in small frying pan. When butter is foaming, add egg mixture, shake pan to spread mixture evenly over base. Cook for 2 minutes over medium heat, lifting edges to allow uncooked egg to flow underneath. When almost set, remove from heat and top with onion and avocado mixture. Sprinkle with cheese. If using bacon, sprinkle bacon over top. Fold omelette in half. Grill for 2–3 minutes or until cheese is melted and golden. Slide onto a warm plate.
4. Mix chilli sauce with water. Drizzle over top of omelette and cut omelette in half. Using an egg slice, place 1 portion on each serving plate. Serve with lettuce and alfalfa sprouts if desired.

Note: As an alternative filling, omit avocado and use combined chopped, fried mushrooms, capsicum and bacon.

Mixed Grated Vegetable Frittata (top) and Avocado and Cheese Omelette.

Pork and Ginger Omelette

Preparation time:
12 minutes
Total cooking time:
18 minutes
Serves 2

1 tablespoon peanut
   oil
375 g finely minced
   lean pork
1 clove garlic, finely
   chopped
2 teaspoons grated fresh
   ginger
1 teaspoon sugar
¹/2 teaspoon salt
¹/2 teaspoon black
   pepper
¹/3 cup water
4 eggs
1 tablespoon soy
   sauce
¹/4 cup finely chopped
   spring onion
soy sauce, additional,
   for serving

1. Heat half the oil in frying pan. Add pork, garlic and ginger. Cook, stirring constantly, until pork breaks into small pieces. Add sugar, salt, pepper and water. Cover and cook over low heat for 6 minutes or until pork is tender. Remove lid from pan, cook until all liquid has evaporated. Allow to cool.

2. Beat eggs with soy sauce. Add cooled pork mixture, stir.
3. Preheat grill. Heat remaining tablespoon of oil in medium frying pan. When hot, pour in the pork omelette mixture. Shake pan to spread mixture evenly over base. Cook over low heat for about 4 minutes or until set at least halfway through. Scatter with spring onion. Place under grill until top has set. Slide onto a plate, serve in wedges with additional soy sauce.

Creamy Zucchini Omelette

Preparation time:
5–10 minutes
Total cooking time:
25 minutes
Serves 2

2 medium zucchini
2 tablespoons olive oil
60 g butter
1 clove garlic, finely
   chopped
5 eggs
2 tablespoons cream
¹/2 teaspoon salt
¹/4 teaspoon pepper
2 tablespoons grated
   parmesan cheese

1. Remove ends from the zucchini and cut horizontally into very thin slices. Melt half the oil and half the butter in a frying pan. Add zucchini and cook, stirring, 2–3 minutes or until zucchini is golden. Sprinkle chopped garlic on top and mix gently. Cook for another 30 seconds. Using a slotted spoon, remove to a plate. Wipe out pan with a paper towel.
2. Beat eggs with cream, salt and pepper. Reheat pan, add remaining oil and butter and when very hot, add eggs. Stir with the back of a fork. Cook for 1 minute, tilting pan and lifting egg edges occasionally to allow uncooked egg to flow underneath.
3. When partly set, spread zucchini evenly over top covering the egg mixture. Reduce heat, cook for 5 minutes or until set around edges. Sprinkle grated parmesan cheese over the top. Cover with a lid and leave omelette to rest in pan for 2 minutes. Slide onto a plate, cut in wedges. May be served with lettuce and capsicum.

Note: Buy parmesan cheese in block form and grate it yourself for a tastier result.

Creamy Zucchini Omelette (top) and Pork and Ginger Omelette.

Chocolate Hazelnut Omelette

Preparation time:
  20 minutes
Total cooking time:
  5 minutes
Serves 4

1/4 *cup finely chopped hazelnuts*
60 g *dark chocolate, roughly chopped*
4 *egg yolks*
1/4 *cup caster sugar*
5 *egg whites*
salt
30 g *unsalted butter*
1 *tablespoon cocoa powder*

1. Stir hazelnuts in dry pan over medium heat until golden. Set aside.
2. Place chocolate in a small heatproof bowl, stand over a pan of simmering water. Stir until melted. Allow to cool slightly.
3. Using an electric beater, beat yolks and sugar for 1 minute or until thick. Add melted chocolate, beat well.
4. Beat whites with a pinch of salt until stiff peaks form. Fold a third at a time into chocolate mixture. Add hazelnuts. Preheat grill.
5. Melt butter in medium frying pan. When butter is foaming pour in chocolate mixture. Swirl pan until mixture evenly covers base. Cook over low heat 1–2 minutes or until set half-way through and bubbles have formed on top. Place under grill, cook until golden. Divide into 4 wedges. Place on serving plates. Dust with sifted cocoa. Serve with vanilla ice-cream and fresh or frozen berries.

Sweet Puffy Bread Omelette

Preparation time:
  20 minutes
Total cooking time:
  5 minutes
Serves 4

1/2 *cup milk*
4 *egg yolks*
2 *tablespoons caster sugar*
1 *teaspoon vanilla essence*
4 *slices white bread, crusts removed, cut in small dice (2 cups)*
2 *egg whites*
45 g *unsalted butter*
icing sugar

Sauce
1/3 *cup sieved apricot jam*
1/3 *cup orange juice*

1. Place milk, egg yolks, caster sugar and vanilla essence in a medium bowl. Mix with a fork until combined. Add bread and stir. Leave to soak for 15 minutes or until bread is soft.
2. In a bowl, beat egg whites until stiff peaks form. Fold one-third at a time into the bread mixture.

20

Chocolate Hazelnut Omelette (left) and Sweet Puffy Bread Omelette.

3. Preheat grill. Melt butter in medium frying pan. Pour in bread mixture. Cook for 2–3 minutes over moderate heat until underside is golden.

Place under grill and heat for 2 minutes or until golden. Slide omelette onto a plate and sift icing sugar over top. Cut into 4 wedges. Place wedges

on serving plates, pour sauce over the top. Serve with cream or ice-cream if desired.
4. *To make sauce:* Heat jam and juice until boiling.

21

Pancakes

Here you will find easy-to-make recipes to tempt family and friends. There are delicious savoury pancakes with fillings such as corn and bacon, mushroom or spinach – excellent for lunch or main meal. Or try sweet pancakes, a favourite with children, served with syrup, jam or fruit, and cream or ice-cream.

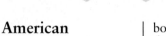

American Hotcakes

Preparation time:
  5 minutes +
  20 minutes standing
Total cooking time:
  1 1/2 minutes per
  hotcake
Makes 9

1 1/2 cups self-raising
  flour
1 teaspoon baking
  powder
2 tablespoons caster
  sugar
pinch salt
2 eggs, lightly
  beaten
1 cup milk
60 g butter, melted
100 g butter, extra
1/2 cup maple syrup

1. Sift flour, baking powder, sugar and salt into a medium mixing bowl; make a well in the centre. Add combined eggs, milk and butter all at once. Using a wire whisk, beat until all liquid is incorporated and batter is free of lumps. Leave, covered with plastic wrap, for 20 minutes.
2. Pour a level 1/4 cup of mixture at a time into lightly greased non-stick pan. Swirl to a circle about 10 cm in diameter. Cook over low heat 1 minute or until underside is golden. Turn hotcake over; cook other side. Transfer to a plate; cover with tea-towel; keep warm.
3. Repeat process with remaining batter, greasing pan when necessary. Serve hotcakes warm or cold with whipped extra

American Hotcakes.

butter and maple syrup.
4. To whip butter for serving, place in small bowl and beat with electric beaters until light and creamy.

Note: If preferred, batter may be prepared in a food processor or blender. Place all ingredients in bowl or container and process until all ingredients are combined and mixture is smooth and free of lumps. Transfer mixture to bowl or jug. Cooked hotcakes can be cooled, covered with plastic wrap, and frozen for up to 3 weeks.

Buttermilk Pancakes with Savoury Mince

Preparation time:
  10 minutes +
  20 minutes standing
Total cooking time:
  25 minutes
Makes 10

500 g beef mince
35 g sachet mild Taco Seasoning Mix
1/4 cup water
200 g jar mild Taco Sauce
290 g can red kidney beans, drained
2 tablespoons finely chopped fresh coriander

Buttermilk Pancakes
2 cups self-raising flour
2 teaspoons caster sugar
2 cups buttermilk
2 eggs, lightly beaten
60 g butter, melted

1. Cook mince in medium, heavy-based pan over high heat for 8 minutes, stirring constantly. Add seasoning mix, stir for 1 minute. Reduce heat to medium, add water, sauce and beans. Stir until mixture reaches the boil. Reduce heat, simmer, uncovered, for 10 minutes, stirring occasionally. Remove from heat, stir in coriander; keep warm.
2. *To make buttermilk pancakes:* Place all ingredients in food processor or blender. Process for 10 seconds or until ingredients are combined and batter is free of lumps. Transfer mixture to a bowl or jug. Leave, covered with plastic wrap, for 20 minutes.
3. Place 1/3 cup of batter at a time into lightly greased non-stick pan; swirl to a circle about 15 cm in diameter. Cook over low heat 2 minutes or until underside is golden. Turn pancake over; cook other side. Transfer to plate; cover with tea-towel, keep

warm. Repeat process with remaining batter, greasing pan when necessary.
4. To serve, cut each pancake into 4 pieces. Arrange overlapping on serving plate. Top with mince in the centre.

Corn and Bacon Pancakes

Preparation time:
  8 minutes +
  20 minutes standing
Total cooking time:
  3–4 minutes per batch
Makes 8

1/4 cup plain flour
1/4 cup self-raising flour
1/2 teaspoon salt
1/4 teaspoon black pepper
2 eggs, lightly beaten
2 tablespoons milk
310 g can creamed corn
2 rashers bacon (100 g), chopped and cooked
2 tablespoons grated parmesan cheese
fresh chives, chopped

1. Sift combined flours, salt and pepper into a medium mixing bowl; make a well in the centre. Add combined eggs and milk all at once. Beat until all liquid is incorporated and batter is free of lumps. Add corn, bacon, cheese and

Buttermilk Pancakes with Savoury Mince (top) and Corn and Bacon Pancakes.

chives, mix well. Leave, covered with plastic wrap, 20 minutes.
2. Pour batter, 2–3 tablespoonsful at a time, into lightly greased frying pan. Cook over medium heat for 2 minutes or until underside is golden. Turn pancakes over, cook other side. Transfer to plate; cover with tea-towel, keep warm.
3. Repeat process with remaining batter, greasing pan when necessary.

Note: These pancakes may be served with sour cream and grated cheddar cheese.

Spinach Pancakes

Preparation time:
  20 minutes +
  10 minutes standing
Total cooking time:
  25 minutes
Makes 7

1/4 *cup self-raising flour*
1/4 *cup plain flour*
1/4 *teaspoon cracked*
  black pepper
pinch salt
pinch ground nutmeg
125 *g frozen spinach,*
  thawed, moisture
  removed, chopped
1/4 *cup grated parmesan*
  cheese
1 *cup milk*
1 *egg, lightly beaten*
1 *cup prepared tomato*
  pasta sauce

Filling
2 *rashers bacon, finely*
  chopped
125 *g frozen spinach,*
  thawed, moisture
  removed, chopped
salt and pepper
3 *eggs, lightly beaten*
1/4 *cup milk*
1/4 *cup grated parmesan*
  cheese

1. Preheat oven to
moderate 180°C. Sift
flours into a medium
mixing bowl. Add
pepper, salt and
nutmeg; make a well in
the centre. Add spinach,
cheese and combined
milk and egg all at

once. Beat until all
liquid is incorporated
and batter is free of
lumps. Leave, covered
with plastic wrap,
10 minutes.
2. Pour 1/4 cup of
mixture into lightly
greased non-stick frying
pan; swirl to a circle
about 14 cm in
diameter. Cook over
low heat 2 minutes
or until underside
is golden. Turn
pancake over and
cook other side.
3. Transfer to plate;
cover with tea-towel,
keep warm. Repeat
process with remaining
batter, greasing pan
when necessary.
4. *To make filling:* Add
bacon to non-stick pan.
Cook over low heat for
5 minutes. Add spinach,
salt and pepper; stir.
Add combined eggs,
milk and cheese. Stir
over low heat with a
wooden spoon until
mixture just begins to
set; remove from heat.
5. Divide filling
between pancakes. Roll
each pancake up tightly.
Arrange filled pancakes
in a shallow ovenproof
dish. Drizzle sauce over
pancakes; heat in oven
10 minutes or until just
warmed through.

Blini

Preparation time:
  25 minutes +
  20 minutes standing
Total cooking time:
  1 minute each blini
Makes 50

3/4 *cup self-raising flour*
pinch bicarbonate of
  soda
pinch salt
1 *teaspoon grated*
  lemon rind
1/3 *cup milk*
1/3 *cup sour cream*
1 *egg, lightly beaten*

Cream Cheese Topping
180 *g cream cheese,*
  softened
1/2 *cup sour cream*
1 *tablespoon finely*
  grated onion
1 *tablespoon lemon*
  juice
1 1/2 *teaspoons ground*
  paprika
1/4 *teaspoon salt*
2 *tablespoons finely*
  chopped fresh parsley

1. Sift flour, soda and
salt into medium
mixing bowl; make a
well in the centre. Add
rind, milk, sour cream
and egg all at once; beat
until mixture is smooth
and free of lumps.
Leave, covered with
plastic wrap, for
20 minutes.
2. Drop mixture, level
teaspoons at at time,

Spinach Pancakes (top) and Blini topped with smoked salmon and sprig of dill.

into lightly greased non-stick frying pan about 2 cm apart; swirl to 3–4 cm rounds.
3. Cook over low heat 30 seconds or until underside is golden. Turn blini over, cook other side. Transfer to plate; cover with tea-towel, keep warm. Repeat process with remaining batter,

greasing the frying pan when necessary.
4. *To make cream cheese topping:* Using electric beaters, beat cheese and sour cream until light and creamy. Add onion and juice; mix well. Add paprika, salt and parsley, beat until well combined.
5. Spread, spoon or pipe cream cheese

topping over blini just before serving. Top with smoked salmon and a sprig of dill if desired.

HINT
Blini can be served with toppings such as curried egg, salmon or lobster pâté or flavoured butters.

27

Crispy Fried Mushroom Pancakes

Preparation time:
  25 minutes +
  20 minutes standing
Total cooking time:
  35 minutes
Makes 12

3/4 cup plain flour
pinch salt
3 eggs, lightly beaten
3/4 cup milk
1 tablespoon light olive oil
2 tablespoons finely chopped fresh chives
2 cups breadcrumbs (made from stale bread)

Mushroom Filling
1 tablespoon olive oil
1 medium onion, finely chopped
400 g mushrooms, finely chopped
1 tablespoon cream
1/4 teaspoon salt
1/2 teaspoon pepper
2 tablespoons grated parmesan cheese

1. Sift flour and salt into medium mixing bowl; make a well in the centre. Add combined eggs and milk all at once. Beat until all liquid is incorporated and batter is free of lumps. Add oil and chives. Leave, covered with plastic wrap, for 20 minutes. Place 1/3 cup of batter in jug; set aside. Pour 2–3 tablespoons remaining batter into lightly greased small crepe pan; swirl evenly over base. Cook over medium heat for 1 minute or until underside is golden. Turn pancake over; cook other side. Transfer to plate; cover with tea-towel, keep warm. Repeat process with remaining batter, greasing pan when necessary.

2. **To make mushroom filling:** Heat oil in frying pan and cook onion over medium heat until soft. Add mushrooms, cook 2–3 minutes. Stir in cream, salt, pepper and cheese. Allow to cool.

3. Place crepes, one at a time, on a plate. Place 1 tablespoonful of mushroom mixture on one half of each crepe, spreading evenly, leaving 1 cm border. Brush edges lightly with some of the reserved pancake batter. Fold uncovered half of crepe over top of mixture. Repeat process until all pancakes are filled. Using a pastry brush, spread a little of the reserved batter over each pancake, sprinkle with breadcrumbs.

Brush top with more batter, mixing with the breadcrumbs.

4. Cover base of large frying pan with oil and heat oil. Add filled pancakes, cook until golden on one side, turn and cook the other side. Transfer to paper towels to drain.

Note: These can be served plain or with a tomato sauce or one of the bottled Italian pasta sauces.

Capsicum and Black Olive Pancakes

Preparation time:
  15 minutes +
  20 minutes standing
Total cooking time:
  15 minutes
Makes 16

2 medium red capsicum
1/2 cup milk
1/2 cup self-raising flour
1/2 teaspoon salt
1/4 teaspoon black pepper
3 eggs, lightly beaten
2 tablespoons finely chopped black olives
1 tablespoon basil, finely chopped
olive oil, for frying

1. Cut each capsicum in half, remove seeds, flatten. Cook capsicum

Crispy Fried Mushroom Pancakes (left) and Capsicum and Black Olive Pancakes.

under grill, skin-side up for 10 minutes or until skin blisters and is black. Cover with a damp tea-towel, allow to cool. Remove skin and chop capsicum flesh roughly.
2. Place capsicum in food processor or blender with milk. Process until smooth.
3. Sift flour with salt into a bowl, add pepper; make a well in centre. Add eggs and capsicum mixture. Stir until combined and mixture is free of lumps. Stir in olives and basil. Leave, covered with plastic wrap, 20 minutes.
4. Brush base of small frying pan with oil. When oil is hot, pour 1–2 tablespoonsful of batter in pan, cook over medium-high heat until underside is golden. Turn over and cook other side. Repeat processs with remaining mixture.

May be served with goats cheese and a sprinkling of fresh herbs.

> **HINT**
> Serve with a side salad for lunch. To reheat, place in greased foil, on top of each other. Seal foil, heat in a moderate 180°C oven for 8–10 minutes or until heated through.

29

Potato and Pumpkin Pancakes

Preparation time:
  25 minutes
Total cooking time:
  25 minutes
Makes 10

250 g potato, cooked
  and mashed
250 g pumpkin, cooked
  and mashed
30 g butter
1/4 cup finely chopped
  spring onions
2 eggs, lightly beaten
1/4 cup plain flour
2 tablespoons self-
  raising flour
1/4 teaspoon ground
  nutmeg
pinch cayenne pepper
1/4 teaspoon salt
30 g butter, extra

1. Place potato and
pumpkin in a food
processor, add butter.
Process until smooth.
Transfer to a bowl, add
spring onion and eggs.
2. Sift flours, spices and
salt into a bowl. Add to
pumpkin mixture; stir
well to combine.
3. Heat the extra butter
in a non-stick frying
pan. Cook heaped
tablespoons of mixture 2
minutes. Turn and cook
for approximately 2–3
minutes or until golden.
Drain on paper towels.
4. Repeat process with
remaining mixture.

Keep warm in oven.
May be served plain or
with yoghurt or butter.

Mexican Cornmeal Pancakes with Avocado

Preparation time:
  20 minutes +
  20 minutes standing
Total cooking time:
  20 minutes
Serves 4–6

1/3 cup yellow cornmeal
  (polenta)
1/2 cup plain flour
1/4 teaspoon baking
  powder
1/4 teaspoon salt
1 teaspoon sugar
1 cup buttermilk
2 eggs
30 g butter, melted
vegetable oil
2/3 cup sour cream, for
  serving

Avocado Mixture
1 large ripe avocado
8 spring onions, finely
  chopped
2 ripe tomatoes,
  finely chopped,
  (discard seeds)
1 teaspoon chilli sauce
  or to taste
2 teaspoons lemon juice
1/4–1/2 teaspoon salt
pepper

1. Sift cornmeal, flour,
baking powder, salt and
sugar into a bowl.
Make a well in the
centre. Place buttermilk,
eggs and butter in a
bowl and beat to
combine. Add to dry
ingredients. Beat until
liquid is incorporated
and batter is free of
lumps. Leave, covered
with plastic wrap,
20 minutes.
2. ***To make avocado
mixture:*** Peel avocado,
remove seed and place
flesh in a bowl. Mash
avocado flesh with a
fork. Add half the
spring onion. Stir in
tomato, chilli sauce,
juice, salt and pepper.
Mix well, chill for
20 minutes.
3. Brush a small frying
pan with oil. When hot,
pour in enough batter
to thinly cover base of
pan. Cook over medium
heat until underside is
golden. Turn pancake
over; cook other side.
Transfer to a plate;
cover with a tea-towel,
keep warm. Repeat
process with remaining
batter, greasing pan
when necessary. Spoon
avocado mixture on
one half of each
pancake, fold over.
Serve each with sour
cream sprinkled with
remaining spring onion.

*Mexican Cornmeal Pancakes with Avocado (top)
and Potato and Pumpkin Pancakes.*

Oatmeal Flapjacks

Preparation time:
  10 minutes +
  10 minutes standing
Total cooking time:
  2 minutes per hotcake
Makes 25

2¹/₂ cups rolled oats
³/₄ cup plain flour
¹/₄ cup caster sugar
³/₄ cup milk
2 eggs, lightly beaten
90 g butter, melted

1. Place 2 cups rolled oats, flour and sugar in food processor or blender. Process for 10 seconds. Add milk, eggs and butter to processor or blender. Process for another 10 seconds or until ingredients are well combined and mixture is free of lumps.
2. Transfer mixture to bowl or jug; stir remaining oats into mixture. Leave, covered with plastic wrap, 10 minutes.
3. Spoon level tablespoons of batter one at a time into lightly greased non-stick frying pan; swirl to a circle about 8 cm in diameter. Cook the flapjacks over low heat for 1 minute or until underside is golden. Turn flapjacks over and cook other side. Transfer to a plate; cover with a tea-towel, keep warm.
4. Repeat process with remaining batter, greasing pan when necessary. Flapjacks may be served with butter and honey or maple syrup.

Spicy Wholemeal Pancakes

Preparation time:
  15 minutes +
  20 minutes standing
Total cooking time:
  2 minutes per pancake
Makes 12

¹/₂ cup self-raising flour
¹/₂ cup wholemeal self-raising flour
2 teaspoons mixed spice
¹/₂ teaspoon cinnamon sugar
3 teaspoons caster sugar
1 cup milk
2 eggs, lightly beaten
2 pears, finely sliced

Spiced Cream
¹/₃ cup sour cream
1 tablespoon honey
¹/₄ teaspoon mixed spice

1. Sift flours, spices and sugar into a medium bowl; make a well in the centre. Add combined milk and eggs all at once. Beat with a wooden spoon until all liquid is incorporated and batter is free of lumps. Leave, covered with plastic wrap, for 20 minutes.
2. Pour 2 level tablespoons of batter at a time into lightly greased non-stick frying pan; swirl to a circle about 12 cm in diameter. Cook over

Oatmeal Flapjacks (left) and Spicy Wholemeal Pancakes.

medium heat for
1 minute or until
underside is golden.
Turn pancake over;
cook other side.
Transfer to a plate,
cover with tea-towel,
keep warm.
3. Repeat process with
remaining batter,

greasing pan when
necessary. Serve with
pears and spiced cream.
May be sprinkled with
cinnamon.
4. *To make spiced
cream:* Combine sour
cream, honey and
mixed spice in a small
bowl. Mix well.

HINT
Use 2 medium
bananas, diagonally
sliced, instead of
pears. Wholemeal
pancakes can also
be served simply
buttered or with a
dollop of yoghurt.

33

Chocolate Pancakes with Macerated Fruits

Preparation time:
  20 minutes +
  20 minutes standing
Total cooking time:
  2 minutes each pancake
Makes 8

Macerated Fruits
1 orange
8 large strawberries,
  quartered
1/2 cup blueberries
1 tablespoon sugar
2 teaspoons white
  crème de caçao liqueur

1 cup self-raising flour
1/4 cup caster sugar
2 tablespoons cocoa
  powder
1 cup milk
1 egg, lightly beaten
30 g butter, melted
1/3 cup thick cream,
  whipped, for serving

1. To make macerated fruits: Place orange on a board. Cut a 2 cm slice off each end of orange down to flesh. Cut skin away in a circular motion, cutting only deep enough to remove all white membrane; discard skin. Separate segments by cutting between membrane and flesh. (Do this over a bowl to catch any juice).

Add strawberries, blueberries, sugar and liqueur to bowl with orange segments and juice. Stir until sugar dissolves; set aside.
2. Sift flour, sugar and cocoa powder into a medium bowl; make a well in the centre. Add combined milk, egg and butter all at once. Beat until all liquid is incorporated and batter is free of lumps. Leave, covered with plastic wrap, for 20 minutes.
3. Pour 1/4 cup of batter at a time into lightly greased non-stick frying pan; swirl to a circle about 12 cm in diameter. Cook over low heat for 1 minute or until underside is golden. Turn pancake over; cook other side. Transfer to a plate; cover with tea-towel, keep warm. Repeat process with remaining batter, greasing pan when necessary. Serve chocolate pancakes with whipped cream and macerated fruits.

French Pancakes

Preparation time:
  20 minutes +
  10 minutes standing
Total cooking time:
  1 minute each pancake
Makes 12

1/2 cup plain flour
2 teaspoons caster sugar
1 cup milk
2 eggs, lightly beaten
60 g butter, melted
1 teaspoon vanilla
  essence
lemon wedges, for
  serving

Sweet Lemon Cream
50 g butter
1/3 cup caster sugar
1/4 cup lemon juice
2–3 tablespoons thick
  cream

1. Place flour, sugar, milk, eggs, butter and essence in food processor or blender. Process for 15 seconds or until ingredients are combined and batter is free of lumps. Transfer mixture to bowl or jug. Leave, covered with plastic wrap, 10 minutes.
2. Pour 2–3 tablespoons batter into lightly greased 20 cm crepe or non-stick pan; swirl evenly over base. Cook over medium heat 30 seconds or until underside is golden. Turn pancake over;

Chocolate Pancakes with Macerated Fruits (top) and French Pancakes.

cook the other side.
Transfer to a plate;
cover with tea-towel,
keep warm.
3. Repeat process with
remaining batter,
greasing pan when
necessary. To serve,

fold each pancake in
half and half again to
form a quarter circle.
Serve drizzled with
sweet lemon cream
and lemon wedges.
4. *To make sweet lemon
cream:* Combine butter,

sugar and juice in small
pan. Stir over low heat
until sugar dissolves
and mixture almost
boils. Add cream, stir
until just heated
through; remove from
heat, serve immediately.

35

Pikelets

Preparation time:
  15 minutes +
  20 minutes standing
Total cooking time:
  1–2 minutes per
  pikelet
Makes 24

1¹/4 *cups self-raising*
  flour
¹/4 *teaspoon bicarbonate*
  of soda
¹/3 *cup caster sugar*
²/3 *cup milk*
2 *eggs, lightly beaten*
20 g *butter, melted*
²/3 *cup thick cream*
²/3 *cup raspberry jam*

1. Sift flour, soda and caster sugar into a medium bowl; make a well in the centre. Add combined milk and eggs all at once. Beat until all liquid is incorporated and batter is free of lumps. Leave, covered with plastic wrap, for 20 minutes.
2. Brush base of a large heavy-based frying pan lightly with melted butter. Drop tablespoons of mixture onto base of pan about 2 cm apart.
3. Cook over low heat for 1 minute or until underside is golden. Turn pikelets over and cook other side. Transfer to a plate; cover with tea-towel, keep warm. Repeat process with remaining batter, greasing pan when necessary. Serve pikelets spread with cream and jam.

Note: It is important to use a flat heavy-based frying pan for making pikelets to ensure even colour and cooking. An electric frying pan is ideal. Pikelets may be served with butter and honey or golden syrup or any of your favourite toppings. They can be stored, refrigerated, and served cold, if preferred.

Hazelnut Pancakes with Chocolate Mousse

Preparation time:
  20 minutes +
  1¹/4 hours
  refrigeration
Total cooking time:
  20 minutes
Makes 8

250 g *dark cooking*
  chocolate, chopped
¹/2 *cup thick cream*
1 *tablespoon soft*
  brown sugar
2 *eggs, separated*
1 *tablespoon Tia Maria*
  liqueur
²/3 *cup cream, for*
  serving
¹/2 *cup chopped roasted*
  hazelnuts, for serving

Hazelnut Pancakes
¹/3 *cup plain flour*
¹/3 *cup self-raising flour*
1 *tablespoon caster sugar*
¹/2 *cup (50 g) ground*
  hazelnuts
1 *cup milk*
2 *eggs, lightly beaten*
30 g *butter, melted*

1. Place chocolate and cream in heatproof bowl. Stand bowl over pan of simmering water, stir until chocolate has melted and mixture is smooth. Cool slightly. Add sugar and lightly beaten egg yolks; beat well. Stir in liqueur. Cover with plastic wrap; refrigerate 15 minutes.
2. Place egg whites in small dry mixing bowl. Using electric beaters, beat egg whites until firm peaks form. Using a metal spoon, fold egg whites into cooled chocolate mixture. Refrigerate 1 hour.
3. *To make hazelnut pancakes:* Sift flours into medium bowl. Add sugar and ground hazelnuts; make a well in the centre. Add combined milk and eggs all at once, beat until mixture is smooth and free of lumps. Stir in butter. Leave, covered with plastic wrap, 10 minutes.
4. Pour ¹/4 cup of mixture into lightly greased non-stick frying pan; swirl to a circle

Pikelets (top) and Hazelnut Pancakes with Chocolate Mousse.

about 15 cm in diameter. Cook over medium heat for 1 minute or until underside is golden. Turn pancake over, cook other side. Transfer to plate; cover with tea-towel, keep warm. Repeat process with remaining batter, greasing pan when necessary.

5. To serve, pipe or spoon some chocolate mousse on half of each pancake; fold pancake over. Place on serving plate, top with cream. Sprinkle with chopped hazelnuts.

HINT
To roast your own hazelnuts, spread nuts on baking tray. Roast in moderate 180°C oven 10–15 minutes. Place nuts on a tea-towel and rub to remove skins.

37

Orange Custard Pancakes

Preparation time:
  20–30 minutes +
  20 minutes standing
Total cooking time:
  20–30 minutes
Serves 8

1/2 cup plain flour
pinch salt
2 eggs, lightly beaten
1/2 cup milk
1/2 teaspoon grated
  orange rind
1/4 cup orange juice
75 g butter
1 1/2 cups milk, extra
1 egg, extra
6 teaspoons custard
  powder
2 tablespoons sugar
1 teaspoon grated
  orange rind, extra
1 tablespoon orange
  liqueur (optional)
45 g butter, extra

1. Sift flour and salt
into a medium bowl;
make a well in the
centre. Add eggs, milk,
orange rind and juice
all at once. Beat until all
liquid is incorporated
and batter is free of
lumps. Melt butter
and mix in. Leave,
covered with plastic
wrap, 20 minutes.
Heat a small frying pan
over medium heat and
melt a little butter. Pour
in 2–3 tablespoons
batter, swirl to coat pan
and cook until
underside is golden.
Turn pancake over,
cook other side.
Transfer to plate, cover
with tea-towel, keep
warm. Repeat process
with remaining batter,
adding butter to pan
when necessary.
2. Heat extra milk in
heavy-based pan until
almost boiling. Remove
from heat. Whisk extra
egg, custard powder,
sugar and rind in
medium heatproof bowl
until mixture forms a
paste. Gradually whisk
in hot milk. Return all
mixture to pan. Stir
over medium heat until
mixture boils and
thickens. Remove from
heat and whisk in
liqueur. Cover surface
with plastic wrap; cool.
3. Lightly grease an
ovenproof dish. Place
pancakes, one at a time,
on a plate. Spoon
2 tablespoons of
custard on each and
fold in ends. Roll over
to enclose and place
each in dish. Melt extra
butter and brush
over pancakes.
4. Preheat oven to
moderate 180°C.
Bake for 15 minutes
or until pancakes are
heated through.

Note: May be served
with fresh orange
segments, and dusted
with icing sugar.

Banana Pancakes with Lemon

Preparation time:
  10 minutes +
  10 minutes standing
Total cooking time:
  3 minutes each batch
Makes 10

2 large bananas,
  mashed (1 cup)
1 tablespoon lemon
  juice
1/4 cup rolled oats
pinch salt
1/2 cup self-raising flour
2 tablespoons caster
  sugar
1 egg, beaten
1/3 cup milk
45 g unsalted butter,
  melted
2 lemons
1–2 bananas, extra
2 tablespoons cinnamon
  sugar

1. Place mashed banana
in a small bowl; stir in
lemon juice.
2. Place rolled oats in
food processor and
process until coarsely
ground. Transfer oats to
medium bowl; add salt,
flour and sugar. Make a
well in the centre. Add
combined egg, milk and
melted butter all at
once. Beat until all
liquid is incorporated
and batter is free of
lumps. Add banana
and mix well. Leave,
covered with plastic

Banana Pancakes with Lemon (top) and Orange Custard Pancakes.

wrap, 10 minutes.
3. Spoon batter,
2 tablespoons at a time,
into lightly greased non-
stick pan. Cook over
medium heat
for 1 minute or until
underside is golden.
Turn pancake over;
cook other side.

4. Squeeze lemon juice
on top of each pancake.
Top with sliced banana
and sprinkle with
cinnamon sugar.

39

Pancakes with Cream Cheese and Cherries

Preparation time:
  30 minutes +
  20 minutes standing
Total cooking time:
  30 minutes
Serves 8

1/2 cup plain flour
pinch salt
1 tablespoon sugar
4 eggs, lightly beaten
1/2 cup milk
30 g butter, melted
450 g jar pitted black or
  red cherries in syrup,
  drained, syrup reserved

Cheese Filling
375 g cream cheese
1/4 cup caster sugar
1/2 teaspoon vanilla
  essence
1 teaspoon grated
  lemon rind
3 teaspoons lemon
  juice

Cherry Sauce
3/4 cup syrup reserved
  from cherries
2 teaspoons cornflour
1 teaspoon rum or
  brandy

1. Sift flour and salt into a medium bowl, add sugar. Make a well in the centre. Add combined eggs and milk all at once. Beat until all liquid is incorporated and batter is free of lumps. Leave, covered with plastic wrap, for 20 minutes.
2. Pour 2–3 tablespoons batter into lightly greased small crepe pan; swirl evenly over base. Cook over medium heat 1–2 minutes or until underside is golden. Transfer to a plate, cover with a tea-towel, keep warm. Repeat process with remaining batter, greasing pan when necessary.

3. *To make cheese filling:* In a small bowl, beat cream cheese until smooth. Add caster sugar, vanilla essence, lemon rind and juice and beat until smooth.
4. Place 2 tablespoons of cheese filling and 4 cherries in the middle of each pancake, fold the sides in and roll up to enclose. Arrange pancakes on individual dishes. Spoon a little of the cherry sauce over the top of each.
To make cherry sauce: Blend 1/4 cup of reserved syrup with cornflour in a small pan. Add rum or brandy and remaining syrup. Stir over medium heat until the mixture boils and thickens. If desired, pancakes may be dusted with icing sugar and served with ice-cream or thick cream.

Pancakes with Cream Cheese and Cherries.

1. Using a wire whisk, beat batter until it is free of lumps.

2. After pouring batter into crepe pan, swirl until base is evenly covered.

3. When cream cheese is smooth, add sugar, essence, rind and juice. Beat again.

4. After placing filling and cherries on pancake, fold sides in and roll up.

Nutty Chocolate Pancake Stack

Preparation time:
  25 minutes +
  20 minutes standing
Total cooking time:
  25 minutes
Serves 6–8

3/4 *cup plain flour*
pinch salt
2 eggs
1 egg yolk
3/4 *cup milk*
30 g butter, melted
vanilla ice-cream, for
  serving

Filling
125 g walnuts
30 g unsalted butter
1/3 *cup caster sugar*
1 teaspoon grated
  orange rind
1 tablespoon orange
  juice
50 g dark chocolate,
  grated

1. Sift flour and salt into a bowl; make a well in the centre. Beat eggs, egg yolk and milk and add to flour all at once. Beat until all the liquid is incorporated and the batter is free of lumps. Stir in melted butter. Leave, covered with plastic wrap, for 20 minutes.
2. Heat a small, lightly greased non-stick frying pan. When pan is hot, pour in 2–3 tablespoonsful of batter; swirl evenly over base. Cook 1–2 minutes or until underside is golden and set. Turn pancake over; cook other side. Transfer to a plate, cover with a tea-towel; keep warm. Repeat process with remaining batter, greasing pan when necessary. Stack pancakes on top of each other.
3. *To make filling:* Finely grind the walnuts in a food processor and add butter, sugar, orange rind and juice. Process until combined. Transfer to a bowl and mix in the grated chocolate. Preheat oven to moderate 180°C.
4. To assemble, place one crepe on base of a buttered pie dish, spread a heaped tablespoon of filling over the crepe. Place a second crepe on top and press down firmly. Repeat process until all the batter and filling have been used, finishing with a crepe. Press down gently.
5. Cover loosely with foil and bake for 5 minutes. Remove foil and cook for another 5 minutes. Remove from oven and leave for a couple of minutes. Cut into wedges; serve with ice-cream. May be served with berries and whipped cream.

Apple Caramel Pancake

Preparation time:
  15 minutes
Total cooking time:
  20 minutes
Serves 4

1 Granny Smith apple,
  peeled and cored
1/3 *cup water*
2 tablespoons soft
  brown sugar
1 tablespoon lemon
  juice
1/2 *teaspoon grated*
  lemon rind
1/4 *teaspoon ground*
  cinnamon
1/4 *cup self-raising flour*
2 eggs, lightly beaten
1/4 *cup milk*
30 g butter
2 tablespoons soft
  brown sugar, extra

1. Cut apple into very small pieces. Place apple and water in a medium frying pan. Cook over medium heat about 8 minutes or until softened and most of the water has evaporated. Add sugar, lemon juice and rind, continue cooking, stirring, for about 10 minutes or until mixture is a caramel colour. Remove pan from heat. Allow apple mixture to cool slightly.
2. Sift cinnamon and flour into a medium

42

Apple Caramel Pancake (top) and Nutty Chocolate Pancake Stack.

bowl and make a well in the centre. Beat eggs with milk and add to flour. Beat until all liquid is incorporated and batter is free of lumps. Add the cooled apple mixture and stir to combine.

3. Preheat grill. Heat butter in frying pan. When butter is very hot, add apple mixture, swirl evenly over base. Cook over a medium heat for about 3–5 minutes until cooked halfway through. Place under grill to cook the top. When set, sprinkle on extra brown sugar. Return to grill and heat until sugar has melted. Cut into quarters and, if desired, serve with whipped cream and mandarin segments.

43

Fritters

A simple batter can be used either to encase foods such as eggplant or scallops or to mix with things such as potato and onion. Deep or shallow fried, they are delicious. Sweet apple or banana can be used for dessert.

Tempura Scallops with Ginger Sauce

Preparation time:
20 minutes
Total cooking time:
3 minutes per batch
Serves 4

Batter
2 egg yolks
3/4 cup iced water
3/4 cup plain flour, sifted

Ginger Sauce
1/2 cup water
1/4 cup white vinegar
1/4 cup soft brown sugar
1 teaspoon sweet chilli sauce
1 tablespoon fresh ginger, grated
1 clove garlic, crushed

500 g scallops
plain flour, extra
oil, for deep-frying

1. *To make batter:* Place yolks in a bowl. Add iced water, mix. Add flour all at once, mix lightly again until just combined. (Batter will be lumpy.)
2. *To make ginger sauce:* In a bowl, combine water, vinegar, sugar, sauce, ginger and garlic.
3. Clean and dry scallops. Place extra flour on a sheet of greaseproof paper and dust scallops in flour. Half fill a medium pan with oil and heat oil to moderately hot. Dip scallops in batter. Using tongs or slotted spoon, lower 3–4 at a time into hot oil and cook until puffed and crisp. Remove and drain on paper towels. Serve with ginger sauce.

Note: Scallops should be served as soon as they are cooked.

Tempura Scallops with Ginger Sauce.

Grated Carrot and Zucchini Fritters

Preparation time:
  20 minutes
Total cooking time:
  3–4 minutes each
  batch
Makes 20

2 medium zucchini,
  grated
1 medium carrot, grated
1 clove garlic, crushed
¹/2 cup grated Jarlsburg
  or cheddar cheese
2 tablespoons finely
  chopped fresh parsley
¹/4 teaspoon salt
freshly ground black
  pepper
¹/3 cup plain flour
olive oil, for frying
¹/4 cup finely grated
  parmesan cheese

1. Cup small handfuls
of zucchini in palm of
hand and squeeze out
excess moisture.
2. Place zucchini,
carrot, garlic, cheese,
parsley, salt and pepper
in a bowl. Sift flour into
same bowl and mix.
3. Heat oil in a pan
until very hot. Place
tablespoonsful of
mixture in 1 hand and
squeeze into an oval
shape. Place in pan and
cook for 1–2 minutes
until fritters are golden

underneath; turn and
cook other side until
just golden. Cook about
5 at a time. Remove
and drain on paper
towels. Repeat with
remaining mixture.
Sprinkle with cheese.

Savoury Italian Rice Fritters

Preparation time:
  35 minutes +
  refrigeration
Total cooking time:
  25 minutes
Makes 10

2 tablespoons olive oil
1 small onion, finely
  chopped
¹/2 cup short grain rice
1¹/4 cups hot chicken
  stock (or stock cube
  and water)
1 clove garlic, crushed
1 tablespoon tomato
  paste
1 teaspoon dried oregano
¹/3 cup freshly grated
  parmesan cheese
30 g butter
2 eggs, beaten
10 x 1 cm cubes of
  cheddar cheese
dry breadcrumbs
oil, extra, for deep-
  frying
1¹/2 cups bottled
  Italian-style tomato
  sauce

1. Heat oil in frying
pan, add onion, cook,
stirring, 5 minutes or
until soft. Add rice,
continue stirring, cook
for another 3 minutes
or until rice is opaque.
2. Pour in half the hot
stock with garlic, tomato
paste and oregano. Bring
mixture to boil, stir
well. When stock has
almost evaporated, add
remaining stock.
Reduce heat, cook
uncovered, for about
10–15 minutes or
until all the liquid is
absorbed. Remove from
heat, stir in parmesan
and butter. Cover with
lid, allow to cool.
3. When cool, add eggs
to rice mixture, stir well.
Place 2 tablespoons of
mixture at a time in
palm of hand. Place
1 cube of cheese in
centre and wrap rice
mixture around to
enclose the cheese.
Form into balls. Place
breadcrumbs on
greaseproof paper.
Roll rice balls in
breadcrumbs.
Refrigerate until firm.
4. Pour enough oil in
a medium, deep pan
to come 3 cm up the
sides; heat oil. Lower
fritters into oil a few
at a time, cook for
4 minutes or until
golden. Remove, drain
on paper towels. Serve
fritters with warmed
tomato sauce.

Savoury Italian Rice Fritters (top)
and Grated Carrot and Zucchini Fritters.

Swedish Potato Fritters

Preparation time:
  15 minutes
Total cooking time:
  4–5 minutes per batch
Makes 10

500 g old potatoes,
  peeled
1 onion, peeled
2 tablespoons plain
  flour
1/2 teaspoon salt
1/2 teaspoon black
  pepper
1 egg, lightly
  beaten
olive oil, for frying

1. Grate potatoes and onion into a bowl. Cup handfuls of mixture in palm of hand and squeeze to remove excess moisture. Discard liquid and return potato and onion to the bowl. Mix until combined. Add flour, salt, pepper and egg to bowl. Mix well.
2. Heat oil in a large frying pan. Place 2 heaped tablespoonsful of the mixture at a time into pan and carefully spread out with the back of a fork to flatten. Cook until underside is brown and crisp. Turn over and cook other side. Drain on paper towels.

Mushroom Fritters

Preparation time:
  20 minutes
Total cooking time:
  15 minutes
Makes 12

12 button mushrooms
1 tablespoon olive oil
1/2 onion, finely
  chopped
1 clove garlic, crushed
1/4 teaspoon salt
1/4 teaspoon black
  pepper
1 teaspoon finely
  chopped fresh thyme
2 eggs, beaten
plain flour
breadcrumbs made
  from stale white bread
oil, extra, for deep-
  frying

Sauce
1/3 cup whole egg
  mayonnaise
1 tablespoon sour
  cream
2 teaspoons lemon juice

1. Remove stalks from mushrooms, chop stalks finely. Heat oil in small pan, add onion and cook over medium heat until soft. Add garlic and mushroom stalks, continue cooking 5 minutes or until mushroom stalks are soft and liquid has evaporated. Remove, season with salt, pepper and thyme. Cool slightly, mix in a tablespoon of egg and spoon a little of the mixture into the cap of each mushroom, pressing in firmly.
2. Place flour on a sheet of greaseproof paper. Place remaining egg in a shallow bowl and the breadcrumbs on another sheet of greaseproof paper. Dust mushroom caps with flour to coat all over; dip in egg and then coat with breadcrumbs, pressing on firmly.
3. Pour enough oil in a pan to come 3 cm up the sides; heat oil. Add mushrooms and cook for 3 minutes or until golden and crisp. Remove and drain on paper towels.
4. *To make sauce:* Mix mayonnaise with sour cream and lemon juice. Serve a little on top of each mushroom.

HINT
Mushrooms may be prepared up to 6 hours ahead and stored, covered, in refrigerator. These fritters can be served as a side dish with barbecued steak or fish.

Mushroom Fritters (top) and Swedish Potato Fritters.

Brain Fritters

Preparation time:
  20 minutes +
  20 minutes soaking
Total cooking time:
  20 minutes
Serves 4

4 sets brains, sliced in
  half
2 cups water
1 bay leaf
1/2 onion, sliced
4 whole peppercorns
2 tablespoons finely
  chopped fresh parsley
1 teaspoon finely
  chopped fresh thyme
1 cup breadcrumbs
  made from stale bread
1/4 cup plain flour
pinch salt
1 egg, lightly beaten
1 teaspoon oil
oil, extra, for deep-
  frying

1. Soak brains in 1 cup
of water for 20 minutes.
Drain brains, discard
water. Peel away as
much skin as possible.
In a pan, heat
remaining water with
brains, bay leaf, onion
and peppercorns and
simmer over low heat
for 15 minutes. Allow
to cool.
2. Combine herbs and
breadcrumbs on a sheet
of greaseproof paper.
Mix flour with salt on a
plate. Mix egg with oil
in a bowl.

3. Dust each brain with
flour, dip in egg mixture
and then coat with
breadcrumbs. Half fill
a medium pan with
extra oil and heat to
moderately hot. Lower
the brains into oil and
fry brains 3 minutes or
until crisp and golden
on the outside. Drain
on paper towels.

Note: Brain Fritters
may be served with
fresh crisp salad
vegetables and lemon
wedges or a little
mustard.

Vegetable and Nut Fritters

Preparation time:
  20 minutes
Total cooking time:
  6 minutes per batch
Makes 8

60 g ground almonds
3/4 cup grated zucchini
3/4 cup grated carrot
1 cup grated pumpkin
2 eggs
1 tablespoon finely
  chopped fresh parsley
1 teaspoon finely
  chopped fresh thyme
1/2 teaspoon salt
1/4 teaspoon black
  pepper
plain flour
oil, for frying

1. Place ground
almonds in a bowl.
Cup handfuls of grated
zucchini in palm of
your hand and squeeze
to remove excess
moisture. Place
squeezed zucchini
in bowl with almonds.
Add grated carrot
and pumpkin and
stir to combine.
2. Place eggs, chopped
parsley and thyme, salt
and pepper in another
bowl and beat until well
combined. Add to
vegetables in bowl and
stir until mixture binds
together. Place rounded
tablespoonsful of
mixture into palm of
hand and form into
balls. Place flour on a
sheet of greaseproof
paper. Roll fritters in
flour until all sides
are coated.
3. Pour enough oil in
a frying pan to come
about 1 cm up the
sides; heat oil to
moderately hot. Add
fritters, flatten slightly
with a fork, cook for
3 minutes over
moderate heat. Turn
fritters over and cook
for 3–4 minutes on the
other side. Do not cook
too quickly as
vegetables must be
cooked through.
Remove and drain on
paper towels. Serve
with a mixed salad.

Vegetable and Nut Fritters (top) and Brain Fritters.

Eggplant Fritters

Preparation time:
  40 minutes +
  20 minutes standing
Total cooking time:
  15–20 minutes
Serves 4–6

Yoghurt Dip
200 g natural yoghurt
2 tablespoons finely
  grated onion
1/2 teaspoon dried mint
  leaves
1/2 teaspoon salt
1/4 teaspoon ground
  coriander
pinch ground cumin

1 large, long eggplant
1 tablespoon salt
2 tablespoons besan
  flour
1/4 teaspoon black
  pepper
1/4 cup self-raising flour
1/2 cup besan flour,
  extra
2 eggs, lightly beaten
1/2 cup cold beer
2 teaspoons lemon juice
2/3 cup olive oil

**1. To make yoghurt
dip:** Beat all ingredients
in a small bowl until
well combined. Cover
bowl with plastic wrap
and refrigerate.
2. Cut eggplant into
20 slices about 5 mm
thick. Sprinkle both
sides of each slice with
salt. Leave to stand in
a colander for about
20 minutes. Rinse the
eggplant under water;
drain well, pat dry with
paper towels.
3. Combine besan flour
and pepper on a sheet
of greaseproof paper.
Dust eggplant lightly in
seasoned flour; shake
off excess.
4. Sift remaining flours
into a medium mixing
bowl; make a well in the
centre. Add eggs, beer
and lemon juice all at
once. Beat until all liquid
is incorporated and
batter is free of lumps.
5. Heat oil in a large
heavy-based frying pan.
Using a fork, dip
floured eggplant into
batter a few pieces at a
time; drain off excess.
Cook eggplant in oil
over medium-high heat
2 minutes or until
underside is golden and
crisp. Turn fritter over
and cook other side.
Transfer to large plate;
keep warm. Repeat
process with remaining
batter and eggplant.
Serve eggplant with
chilled yoghurt dip.

Note: Besan flour is
made from ground
lentils, and is yellow in
colour. It is available in
health food stores and
specialty delicatessens.
Eggplant can be cut
into thick batons if
preferred, before
salting, rinsing
and drying.

Corn Fritters

Preparation time:
  15 minutes
Total cooking time:
  3 minutes each batch
Makes 20

1 1/4 cups plain flour
1 1/2 teaspoons baking
  powder
1/2 teaspoon ground
  coriander
1/4 teaspoon ground
  cumin
130 g can corn kernels,
  well drained
130 g can creamed corn
1/2 cup milk
2 eggs, lightly beaten
2 tablespoons chopped
  fresh chives
salt and pepper
1/2 cup olive oil

Dipping Sauce
1 tablespoon brown
  vinegar
3 teaspoons soft brown
  sugar
1 teaspoon sambal
  oelek or chilli sauce
1 tablespoon chopped
  fresh chives
1/2 teaspoon soy sauce

1. Sift flour, baking
powder, ground
coriander and cumin
into a medium bowl;
make a well in the
centre. Add corn
kernels, creamed corn,
milk, eggs, chives, salt
and pepper all at once.
Stir until ingredients are

Eggplant Fritters (top) and Corn Fritters.

combined and mixture is free of lumps.
2. Heat oil in a large non-stick pan. Drop heaped tablespoonsful of mixture into pan about 2 cm apart, flatten slightly. Cook over medium-high heat 2 minutes or until underside is golden. Turn fritters over and cook the other side. Remove from pan, drain on paper towels; repeat process with remaining mixture. Serve fritters with the dipping sauce.
3. *To make dipping sauce:* Heat brown vinegar, sugar, sambal oelek, chives and soy sauce in a small pan for 1–2 minutes until heated through and sugar is dissolved.

53

Cheese Fritters

Preparation time:
  15 minutes +
  25 minutes standing
Total cooking time:
  10 minutes
Serves 4–6

175 g block firm fetta
  cheese
125 g mozzarella cheese
1/3 cup plain flour
1/4 teaspoon black
  pepper
1 egg, lightly beaten
1/2 cup dried
  breadcrumbs
oil, for deep-frying

1. Cut fetta and
mozzarella into 2 cm
cubes. Combine flour
and pepper on a sheet
of greaseproof paper.
Toss cheese lightly in
seasoned flour, shake
off excess.
2. Dip cheese into egg a
few pieces at a time.
Coat with crumbs;
shake off excess. Repeat
process with remaining
cheese and crumbs.
Arrange cheese on foil-
lined tray. Refrigerate,
covered, 25 minutes.
3. Pour enough oil in a
medium, deep pan to
come 3 cm up the sides;
heat oil to moderately
hot. Add cheese a few
pieces at a time. Cook
over a medium heat 2–3
minutes or until golden
and crisp.

4. Remove from pan,
drain on paper towels.
Repeat process with
remaining cheese. Serve.

HINT
Serve cheese fritters
as a snack or a first
course with sweet
chilli, plum or
cranberry sauce
or warmed mint
jelly if desired.

Seafood Fritters

Preparation time:
  10 minutes
Total cooking time:
  8 minutes
Makes 20

2 spring onions, finely
  chopped
200 g can crab meat,
  well drained
200 g can peeled
  prawns, well drained
2 teaspoons lemon juice
pinch salt
1 egg, lightly beaten
2/3 cup self-raising flour,
  sifted
1/3 cup cold beer
2/3 cup oil
1/2 cup sweet chilli sauce

1. Place spring onion,
crab meat, prawns,
lemon juice, salt and
beaten egg in a medium
bowl; stir with a
wooden spoon.
2. Add flour and beer
all at once. Beat until all

ingredients are combined
and mixture is smooth.
3. Heat oil in large
heavy-based frying pan.
Place tablespoonsful
of mixture at a time in
pan about 2 cm apart;
flatten slightly.
4. Cook over medium-
high heat 2 minutes or
until underside is
golden. Turn fritters
over, cook other side.
Transfer to plate; keep
warm. Repeat process
with remaining mixture.
Serve fritters with sweet
chilli sauce.

Cheese and
Parsley Puffs

Preparation time:
  20 minutes
Total cooking time:
  20 minutes
Makes 45

60 g butter, chopped
1/2 cup water
2/3 cup plain flour
pinch of salt
pinch of cayenne pepper
3 eggs, lightly beaten
3/4 cup coarsely grated
  parmesan cheese
1/2 teaspoon cracked
  black pepper
1/4 cup coarsely chopped
  fresh parsley
oil, for deep-frying

1. Combine butter and
water in medium pan.
Stir over low heat until

Clockwise from top: Seafood Fritters, Cheese Fritters, Cheese and Parsley Puffs.

butter has melted. Bring mixture to boil.
2. Remove pan from heat, add combined flour, salt and cayenne all at once. Using a wooden spoon, beat until smooth. Return to stove, heat 2 minutes or until mixture thickens and comes away from sides and base of pan. Remove from heat; transfer mixture to food processor.

3. With motor running, add eggs all at once. Process 1 minute or until mixture is smooth and glossy. Add cheese, pepper and parsley all at once. Process for 10 seconds or until all ingredients are just combined. Transfer mixture to small bowl.
4. Pour enough oil in a medium, heavy-based, deep pan to come 3 cm up the sides; heat oil to

moderately hot. Carefully drop tablespoonsful of mixture at a time into oil. (Cook about 6 at a time over medium heat).
5. Cook puffs, turning frequently using a slotted spoon, for about 5 minutes or until puffs are brown and crisp. Remove from oil with slotted spoon; drain on paper towels. Serve.

Dutch Minced Meat Fritters

Preparation time:
40 minutes +
refrigeration
Total cooking time:
20 minutes +
3 minutes per batch
Makes 24

2 tablespoons olive oil
1 large onion, finely
   chopped
1 clove garlic, finely
   chopped
45 g butter
1 tablespoon curry
   powder
2 tablespoons plain
   flour
3/4 cup milk
1 tablespoon mango or
   tomato chutney
1/4 teaspoon salt
1/4 teaspoon black
   pepper
2 cups firmly packed
   minced, cooked, cold
   lamb, beef or chicken
plain flour

2 eggs
breadcrumbs made
   from stale bread
oil, extra, for deep-frying
mango or tomato
   chutney, extra, for
   serving

1. Heat oil in a pan,
add onion and cook
until golden and soft.
Add garlic, cook for
30 seconds. Melt butter
in pan. Add curry
powder and fry until
aromatic, add plain
flour and stir 2 minutes.
Remove from heat.
Gradually add milk and
stir constantly until
smooth. Return to
stove. Stir constantly
over medium heat until
mixture boils and
thickens. Add chutney,
salt and pepper. Remove
from heat and add meat
stirring until all mince is
moist with sauce. Allow
to cool, cover with
plastic wrap; refrigerate

for at least 1 hour.
2. Using wet hands, form
heaped tablespoonsful of
mixture into balls.
3. Place flour on a
plate. Beat eggs in a
shallow bowl. Place
breadcrumbs on a sheet
of greaseproof paper.
Coat the balls in flour,
shake off excess, dip in
egg and coat with
breadcrumbs. Cover
and refrigerate for
1 hour or overnight.
4. Half fill a large pan
with oil and heat oil to
moderately hot. Lower
meatballs into hot oil,
a few at a time, making
sure they are covered
with oil. When golden
and crisp, remove from
oil with a slotted spoon;
drain on paper towels.
Serve with chutney.

Note: Use any leftover
roast meat. Mince it in
food processor or cut
finely with sharp knife.

Dutch Minced Meat Fritters.

1. Add minced meat to pan. Stir until all
the mince is coated with sauce.

2. Measure heaped tablespoonsful of
mixture into hand and form into balls.

3. Coat balls in flour, dip in egg and then coat thoroughly with breadcrumbs.

4. Using a slotted spoon, remove fritters from oil and drain on paper towels.

Russian Cream Cheese Fritters

Preparation time:
  20 minutes +
  refrigeration
Total cooking time:
  4 minutes per batch
Makes 14

500 g fresh cream
  cheese or ricotta
  cheese
2 egg yolks
pinch salt
2 tablespoons caster
  sugar
1 teaspoon grated
  lemon rind
plain flour
45 g butter
2 tablespoons oil
2 lemons
2 tablespoons icing
  sugar
1/2 cup sour cream or
  plain yoghurt

1. Mash cream cheese
or ricotta with a fork.
Add egg yolks, salt,
sugar and lemon rind,
stir well. Refrigerate for
several hours or up to
24 hours.
2. Place flour on a
plate. Drop heaped
tablespoonsful of cheese
mixture onto flour,
turning gently to coat
well. Shake off excess.
Form into a ball and
flatten slightly.

3. Heat half the butter
with half the oil in
medium frying pan.
Add fritters to the pan
about 2 cm apart. Cook
over medium heat for
2–3 minutes or until
underside is golden.
Turn over and cook the
other side. Drain on
paper towels. Repeat
process, heating
remaining butter and
oil as needed. Squeeze
lemon juice over the
top. Sprinkle with sifted
icing sugar and serve
with sour cream or
yoghurt, if desired.

Banana Fritters

Preparation time:
  10 minutes
Total cooking time:
  3 minutes
Serves 4

3 large firm, ripe
  bananas
2 tablespoons plain
  flour
1 egg, lightly beaten
1/2 cup dried
  breadcrumbs
2 tablespoons ground
  almonds
1/2 teaspoon ground
  cinnamon
60 g butter
1 tablespoon oil
2/3 cup cream
icing sugar

1. Line a tray with
greaseproof paper. Cut
bananas in half
horizontally and then in
half again lengthways.
Toss banana lightly in
flour; shake off excess.
Dip banana in egg a few
pieces at a time. Coat
with combined
breadcrumbs, almonds
and cinnamon; shake
off excess. Arrange
crumbed pieces on tray.
2. Heat butter and oil in
large heavy-based frying
pan. Add bananas in
single layer. Cook over
medium heat 2 minutes
or until underside is
golden. Turn fritters
over and cook other
side for 1 minute.
Remove from pan,
drain on paper towels.
3. Dust banana fritters
lightly with icing sugar
and serve warm. Serve
with ice-cream,
if desired.

Note: Bananas are best
prepared just before
serving to prevent
discolouration.
Serve banana fritters
  with your favourite
  flavoured sauce.

*Banana Fritters (top) and Russian Cream Cheese
Fritters.*

Sweet Rice and Currant Fritters

Preparation time:
20 minutes
Total cooking time:
3 minutes per batch
Makes 12

¹/₃ cup currants
2 tablespoons lemon
  juice
1 teaspoon grated
  lemon rind
2 eggs, separated
1 egg yolk
pinch salt
¹/₃ cup plain flour
1 tablespoon caster
  sugar
²/₃ cup cooked long-
  grain rice
30 g butter
2 tablespoons sugar
¹/₄ teaspoon ground
  cinnamon

1. In a small bowl, combine currants with lemon juice and rind.
2. Place the 3 egg yolks in a large bowl. Add salt, flour and caster sugar; beat until combined. Add rice and currants with juice.
3. In a small, dry bowl, beat egg whites until stiff peaks form. Fold one-third into rice mixture. Gradually fold in the remaining egg white.
4. Heat butter in a frying pan. Add tablespoonsful of the rice mixture at a time, swirl pan until mixture forms small circles. Cook over low heat for about 2 minutes, turn and cook other side for 1–2 minutes or until golden brown and cooked through.
5. Serve plain or sprinkled with combined sugar and cinnamon.

Ice-cream Fritters

Preparation time:
40 minutes + freezing
Total cooking time:
12 minutes
Makes 12

1 litre vanilla ice-cream
450 g madeira loaf cake
2 eggs, lightly beaten
¹/₂ cup dried
  breadcrumbs
¹/₄ cup desiccated
  coconut
¹/₄ teaspoon mixed spice
oil, for deep-frying
strawberries, for serving

Caramel Sauce
60 g butter
¹/₂ cup soft brown sugar
2 teaspoons cornflour
¹/₃ cup sour cream
1 teaspoon lemon juice

1. Dip a small metal ice-cream scoop into warm water; shake off excess. Use scoop to form ice-cream into a ball. Place ice-cream ball on a foil-lined tray. Repeat process with scoop, water and

ice-cream until 12 balls are formed. Return ice-cream balls to freezer for 1 hour or until firm.
2. Trim madeira cake of dark brown edge. Cut cake into 18 slices of even thickness. Cut 6 slices in half. Place 1 slice of cake into palm of hand. Place an ice-cream ball in centre of cake piece; top ball with a half slice of cake.
3. Working quickly, (gently but firmly) using wet hands, shape cake around the ice-cream

Sweet Rice and Currant Fritters (left) and Ice-cream Fritters.

until it is well sealed and fully enclosed. Return each ball to freezer; repeat process with remaining cake and ice-cream balls.

4. Dip balls into beaten egg one at a time. Coat with combined breadcrumbs, coconut and spice; shake off excess. Repeat process with remaining egg and crumb mixture. Return balls to freezer.

5. Half fill a small, deep heavy-based pan with oil and heat oil to moderately hot. Using a metal spoon, gently lower ice-cream balls into oil, about 2–3 at a time. Cook over medium-high heat for 2 minutes or until golden and crisp. Carefully remove from oil with a slotted spoon and drain on paper towels. Serve with caramel sauce and sliced strawberries.

6. *To make caramel sauce:* Place butter, sugar, cornflour, sour cream and juice in small heavy-based pan. Stir constantly over low heat for 3 minutes or until butter melts and sugar is dissolved. Bring to boil, reduce heat, stir until mixture boils and thickens. Remove from heat, cool slightly.

Note: Crumbed ice-cream balls can be stored in an airtight container in freezer for up to 1 month.

Pineapple Fritters

Preparation time:
  10 minutes +
  20 minutes standing
Total cooking time:
  10 minutes
Makes 6

450 g can pineapple
  rings, drained
1/2 cup self-raising flour
1 teaspoon sugar
1/2 cup cold soda water
1 egg, lightly beaten
oil, for deep-frying

1. Place pineapple rings
onto paper towels to
drain well.
2. Sift flour and sugar
into small mixing bowl.
Make a well in the
centre. Add water
and egg all at once.
Beat until all liquid is
incorporated and
mixture is free of
lumps. Leave, covered
with plastic wrap,
20 minutes.
3. Pour enough oil in
a medium, deep pan to
come 3 cm up the sides;
heat oil. Dip one
pineapple ring at a time
into batter, using tongs
or a fork, coating both
sides. Gently lower 2–3
rings at a time into hot
oil. Cook over medium
heat for 4 minutes or
until golden and crisp.
Carefully remove rings
from oil with tongs or a
slotted spoon. Drain on
paper towels. Repeat
process with remaining
pineapple and batter.
4. Serve pineapple
fritters with crisp, fried
chicken and chips or,
if preferred, as dessert
with banana fritters
and cream.

Apple Fritters

Preparation time:
  10 minutes
Total cooking time:
  18 minutes
Serves 4

1/4 cup cornflour
1/2 teaspoon sugar
1 tablespoon toasted
  sesame seeds
1 egg white, lightly
  beaten
1 tablespoon iced water
2 green apples, peeled,
  cut into eight wedges
oil, for deep-frying
1 tablespoon toasted
  sesame seeds, extra,
  for serving

Syrup
2/3 cup sugar
2 tablespoons water
1 teaspoon lemon juice

1. Place cornflour,
sugar and seeds into
small bowl; make a well
in the centre. Add egg
white and water. Beat
until all liquid is
incorporated and
mixture is free of lumps.
2. Pour enough oil in a
medium, deep pan to
come 3 cm up the sides;
heat oil. Add apples a
few at a time to batter,
stir with a fork until
well coated. Remove,
drain off excess batter
and gently lower apples
into hot oil with a fork.
3. Cook over medium-
high heat for 3 minutes
or until golden and
crisp. Remove apples
from oil with tongs or
slotted spoon. Drain on
paper towels. Repeat
process with remaining
apples and batter.
4. Transfer apples to
serving plate, drizzle
with syrup, sprinkle
with extra seeds.
5. *To make syrup:*
Combine sugar, water
and juice in small
heavy-based pan. Stir
over low heat for
5 minutes or until sugar
dissolves. Bring to boil,
reduce heat; simmer,
uncovered, without
stirring, for 8 minutes
or until syrup is light
golden in colour.
Remove from heat
immediately; leave to
stand for 1 minute.

Note: Syrup and fritters
are best made just
before serving. Serve
with baked or grilled
pork or as a dessert
with ice-cream.

Pineapple Fritters (top) and Apple Fritters.

Index